Measured in Heart Rate

Measured in Heart Rate

A Mini Collection of Poetry

Madeline Mitchell

Published by Tablo

Copyright © Madeline Mitchell 2020.
Published in 2020 by Tablo Publishing.

All rights reserved.

This book or any portion thereof may not be reproduced or used in any manner whatsoever without the express written permission of the author except for the use of brief quotations in a book review.

Publisher and wholesale enquiries: orders@tablo.io

20 21 22 23 LSC 10 9 8 7 6 5 4 3 2 1

In memory of Jess Burns and my beloved donor.
Two beautiful hearts that changed my life for the better.

One

Sometimes it feels like the world is an ocean and our hearts are meant to be glass bottles of untouched emotions that drift across the sea. Devotion to romanticizing silence has been illustrated and rolled up inside like a hidden treasure map or a love letter but the beauty in unexpressed feelings never really spoke to me.

An open book is how I see myself - picked up and looked at hundreds of times with eyes that offer different perspectives, but not many ever take more from it than what is offered at first glance, mixed with a teaspoon of their preconceived notions and very little acquaintance.

When looked at by someone else, my lips will quiver but my heart will dance and tell the stories of the mountains I've had to climb and how the climax is falling to my death and forgetting what it feels like to be alive.

Truthfulness is a flavor that is acquired but I've come to discover that having a room full of people inspired isn't worth dipping my lines of poetry in lies so that the words swallowed have a sweet aftertaste everyone wants to savor.

If our hearts are meant to be glass bottles, mine is shattered and held together with duct tape that hardly covers the cracks, letting every feeling ever felt spill in and out, but I sure as hell no longer have any doubt that my losses will take me through a different wave instead of lifeless inside a boat. I will never be the superhero with the cape who's been sent to save the day but the world is my ocean and the riptides will always be a beautiful commotion.

Two

He told me his middle name was rain. He kissed my lips in a torrential downpour on a Tuesday outside a bookstore.

From time to time, I blame myself when poetry fails me and I can't articulate the storms that rolled in months and years later.

But the atmosphere has a way of expressing what seems to be on the tip of my tongue but I can never quite put my finger on.

And sometimes

When the sky is overwhelmed with frustration

I'd like to settle into the clouds, wrap myself up in thunder, hold the lighting in my arms

And say

"Thank you for understanding what I can't put into words."

Three

Welcome to the fun house
Step right up and see
A maze of misconceptions
Disguised as reality

First you'll walk a hall
With a row of distorted mirrors
The reflection of others pass you by
But yours could not be clearer

Don't let the colors fool you
Or you'll fall into their trap
And if you start to lose yourself
They won't give you a map

Your view is delicately sculpted
Into a carefully made mess
Everything you think you know
You'll always second guess

An emotional obstacle course
With no end in sight
Some will run through every part
In hopes to see the light

But hearts are beneath the surface
Where they have lived and grown
So be careful what you step on
It could just be your own

Four

You were the drug that lingered in my cabinet
Past your expiration date

You were the relief that sedated me
With broken promises and hand stitched fate

Every time I would get clean
You somehow showed up again

You were the exception to a sobriety
I had always tried to bend

I forgot the side effects of your toxicity
That I'd heard a hundred times before

You were my pain killer but I overdosed on you
Now I'm as empty as the pill bottle on the floor

I guess I was addicted

To the rise before the fall

I don't know what's worse

The high or the withdrawal

Five

I have met heartbreak before. She has showed up on my doorstep when boys kissing me goodnight told white lies. She has dripped down my face from the tears in my eyes with the words "I don't love you anymore" scribbled across a screen. I have seen her whisk away love in a matter of seconds.

But with you it was different. You were a slow burn disguised as a constellation being followed for direction. I didn't realize back then that even stars can blaze like the sun on a hot summer day. I was so blinded by your brightness that I didn't notice the scars you left on my heart until they started to fade alongside your presence. I wanted you to stay. We made sense together and five broken years was not the forever I imagined for us. We must have fallen apart at least a hundred times but we always made our way back to each other. I gave you everything of mine to keep your flame alive. She was the art hanging on your wall but I was the light that let you see it in the first place. I was a masterpiece that simply went to waste. I'm smart enough to know that the distance was too far for you regardless of how close we had become. Heartbreak may be cold, but yours was a sunburn.

What we had was sparks but I never stopped to heal the very skin I let you hold a lighter to. When you set my heart on fire and burned her down I could only desire you telling me how much she had glowed. I looked for our remains in all different ways and I'm not sure if I was hoping to find yours or my own.

I'm just the kid who touched the stovetop, but I never learned how to pull my hand away.

Six

Losing you to the universe felt like I was a crystal vase that had just shattered into a million pieces. At first, your disappearance only increased the hope that somehow you'd make a reappearance. Now I know that trying to bargain with the night sky were the words of mourning a losing battle. Anyone who thinks you lost the fight doesn't realize that you are eternally undefeated. You're a light who didn't deserve the darkness of pain you went through. People say when you leave you gain angel wings, but for you it's untrue. The way you treated others proved you had them from the beginning and will for the infinity of time.

When your lungs couldn't work I wanted to give you mine. I'm locked in a room, where I am reminded I lived but you died so soon. It's not fair that someone so young and full of passion was given limited air. I would say I wish the afterworld had a phone so I could call you and hear your words once more, but once wouldn't ever be enough. I have never known someone to be as tough as you are.

To my heart you are close, but to my soul you are far. Most days I think about the thought of you being next to me. Every so often I can almost touch the love you've given and the wisdom you've taught. There are days I could swear that I caught your reflection in the mirror and I realize there are parts of you that will survive forever. My glass may be broken but there will never be a moment that I can't hold every single blessing you've given me. But since you've left this world, it will always feel somewhat empty.

Seven

The night sky is painted with glimmering stars
For a moment I seem to forget where we are
An existence based on judgmental speculation
Where peace is only found in death and meditation

In a society that functions from being attached to
Capitalism and fame instead of morals and values
The concept that beauty is based off a weight
From a fluctuating scale and not the artwork we create

Healing orbits around broken bones and sprains
But a more complex illness cannot be explained
Except through antidepressants and talk therapy
Until it's determined what's needed is heart surgery

In a world where all that really seems to matter
Is confident insecurity and meaningless chatter
Earth is the essence of an unfamiliar tour
That I can't recognize but I've traveled before

This simply could be a rest stop we're passing
While the planets off in the distance are laughing
As we continue to wander and roam
The minuscule bubble we like to call home

Eight

This heart contradicts my soul. Only one ever seems to grow old. Five years later and you are still the face that is etched into my brain.

This heart contradicts my soul. Loving you takes its toll on me. Fairy dust ventures through my veins and the weight of a thousand tears flow through my arteries.

This heart contradicts my soul. Your body is warm but your mind is ice cold. You are the boy in the blue jacket with a blue essence to match it.

This heart contradicts my soul. Loving you leaves me breathless. Take the mess that is beating inside my chest, and run while I lay there, running out of air.

Nine

What would you say
If I told you my breath was taken away
A person I love, you would probably assume
But I was gasping for air in a hospital room
Where death sat at the edge of my bed
And said
"I have your bags packed, I promise you'll be fine"
Flashing a one way ticket to a blaring flatline

What would you say
If I told you my heart was torn out of my chest
Heartbreaking news would be your best guess
But I was cut open with the blade of a scalpel
Pumped with chemicals as I went into battle
An expedition through broken sternal wires
Where an overworked heart was overly tired
The removal of a roaring humidifier
Replaced with the glow of a strong inner fire

What would you say
If I told you my body has prepared me to die
You'd argue we all will, but wouldn't grasp why
It's invalidating to compare our mortality as support
For a life that I live that is already short

Metaphors can be tricky you see
But you'll understand, if you're anything like me
That our hearts have been through a deep violent war
It is the fight that prepares us
To go back for more

Ten

The feeling of pain crashed over her body like a tidal wave. They were able to reset the timer inside her but couldn't save her from the timeless turmoil inside her brain. Antibodies were only a threat to what now masked a permanent stain.

She tried to forget while the memories rushed through her bloodstream. They say rain is followed by rainbows but no one warned her that afterwards would be crossbows. There were never any dreams, merely a dose of elaborate hallucination and the reality she could only wish was.

Because how is it fair that air would swish freely throughout tubes, while her body was so broken that she couldn't even move? The books from medical school may have taught chemistry, but not once did they mention the element being fought for in desperation to survive. It seems sedation and loss of identity is what's given to those who are barely alive.

The cost of her ability is what left her in debt. She had to pay with vulnerability and trusting people she's never met. Once hopeful but then full of regret from walking into the arms of assault and neglect. Feeling broken beyond repair like a mirror that was cracked. Healing seems nonexistent after being attacked. Although reflecting instead of rejecting is how her heart went on inside. It's when recovery was born and giving up had died.

Eleven

I remember the first time you kissed me. It was in a busy hallway against the wall. I felt dizzy with love and was knocked off my feet. The shock of the moment was what numbed the fall.

All I ever wanted was someone to catch me. Maybe we weren't a match made in heaven, but god did I want us to be. Almost seven months encapsulated in your protection and a lifetime of your reflection in every brunette mess I'd see.

I took the potential inner love I had and put it on a shelf. Who would have guessed that working on your reconstruction was a coverup of the deconstruction to myself?

You traced your finger down the crevice that held the markings of my scar. It was the flesh above a graveyard where a broken heart was buried. I spilled the last drop of love on what was destined to break apart because you found someone else and decided to get married.

Letting go of you was hard but letting go of what I loved you with was harder. Your departure was brief and didn't offer any closure. It wasn't until they sewed my chest shut that I realized the healing would be more painful than the cut.

Perhaps it's a relief that the feeling of your absence is the silence stirred in with chaos that gives my life a little balance.

Twelve

Before our introduction, the plans to meet you were an interruption to my life. Prom dresses turned into hospital gowns and graduation was celebrating that I had outgrown the sound inside my chest, rather than the halls walked through where knowledge was borrowed. Our connection was initiated from the broken promise of your tomorrow.

There is no poetry that could ever transform your family's sorrows or my own survivor's guilt into words. It is a blessing and a tragedy to share my life with yours. I may not be the recipient who runs 5K races or marathons but I will bring you on a journey of self love and forgiveness. Fitness will not be at the top of the list but I will make sure you live through each moment you missed.

I will show you heartbreak and then tell you that the worst of it is not from falling in love but forgetting to save some for yourself. I will teach you to take a look in the mirror and not fear her so-called imperfections, because intentions are the beauty masked by misunderstood reflections. I will let you know everything I wish I'd been told when I was twelve years old.

The promise of your tomorrow may have been broken but to you mine is open. I will listen to you through each breath that is spoken. I will treasure your spirit and take care of your heart. I will love you like I should have loved myself from the start.

Thirteen

When I was a kid, they asked me what three things I would bring if I were stranded on a desert island. I wasn't sure how to answer, because how could I when part of me was already there? How was I supposed to tell them that I was isolated with nothing but my bones to start a fire and scar tissue to dry my tears with when it finally burned out?

When doctors would say I was out of the woods, they didn't realize that I had built my home out there. That I spent my existence trudging through the shattered pieces of my own heart and soul. It took so long to find me that by the time they did, I had already grown accustomed to living in the dark.

It's easy to claim something is fixed when you're not the one holding it together. I am someone who came into this world with a broken heart. I now have one that is whole, but what people fail to realize is that I had to be cracked open beyond the damage I was made with to receive it. I am not a puzzle that can be connected to create something beautiful. I had to paint the picture for myself with the blood inside me that swirled with red and blue. I took my sadness and rage and turned it into a garden of violets and roses.

I am a creature born out of the darkness and I say that proudly. The leaves and twigs entangled in my hair are roots that cannot simply be combed out. I am moving on to become someone who is seen in the light of day but I will never forget where I came from. I will never forget who raised me.

Fourteen

You created a wall that's been designed over the years with every brick in mind as you enclosed yourself.

When you spend enough time barricaded inside your own defense mechanisms, you start believing that's all there is.

You are allowed to cry as you take a hammer and smash the structure you've built with your own hands.

Allowing yourself this freedom doesn't erase the years of pain. But it will lead you to an existence of love being stronger than fear.

Just remember that as the bricks come tumbling down, it will hurt. But you will finally feel the wind in your hair and the sun on your face.

And little by little as you become more whole, you'll realize that you are more powerful than any fortification.

The sanctuary you've been searching for is discovered. You carry it in your heart every day and it's already beaming among your bones.

You may not always be able to find it. But it will always be able to find you.

Fifteen

Sometimes I think about little me and how she would handle this year. I'm pretty sure she would crumble from all the anxiety.

And if I'm honest, I've been crumbling myself.

But this time

I'm not afraid to scoop up the parts that I was once too scared to look at

And realize that even when I fall apart I will still be left with stardust.

Don't worry little me, the universe is infinite

And the cosmos will never leave you empty handed.

Sixteen

It's not your job to heal the source that broke you to begin with.

It is you who needs to wrap your heart and heal it with time.

When the cast comes off you will finally let it soak under the rain and cherish the way it loves like never before.

Just because something broke you, doesn't mean you'll stay that way.

Seventeen

Sometimes I want to get a tattoo to symbolize my story through art. I want to admire the words and pictures I've accepted to proudly show the world.

But then I realized that I have my own. I didn't chose to receive mine but I recognize the strength from how they were given to me.

The needle drew blood instead of ink. My forever tainted skin may not create a beautiful picture but the meaning behind it will always hold beauty from winning a battle.

And that is art within itself.

Eighteen

I will never forget the very day I first met you.
Your radiant smile from the bed in a hospital room.

I will never forget when you held me in your arms.
Wrapped up in blankets & love as you protected me from harm.

I will never forget the beauty you gave my life.
You brought spoons of hope when I went under the knife.

I will never forget that only you could understand.
You knew pain and suffering, so you offered me your hand.

I will never forget you through the laughter and the tears.
Because while I miss you terribly, I know that you're still here.

Nineteen

I wallowed through the halls in solitude as my shadow eloquently danced under the skylight. The mystery of what is yet to be fell upon me as the glimmering darkness swept me into its embrace.

The future has a humble way of looming presence over the past. Curiosity will drip-drop into my mind like a drizzle. And while yesterday may foreshadow tomorrow, today will always lock their lips and throw away the key.

Don't ask me if I'm afraid of what's next to come. I'm only scared of certainty.

After all, it is the unknown that is the most beautiful.

Twenty

In literary terms, one could say I died a thousand deaths when he let go of my hand. Each time he took it into his own, I could feel the defibrillators shock my heart back into rhythm and the electricity struck my bones like lightning.

Little did I realize that these internal paddles weren't infallible. The slightest miscommunication could set off a bomb inside my chest cavity. Within the home that's been caged for over a decade.

So tell me, why am I lying in a hospital bed surrounded by oxygen tanks and I still can't breathe? Who broke my sternum, and told me to let it heal?

There is no instruction book on how to survive heart surgeries or boys with green and blue eyes who you accidentally fall in love with. You just get tossed into the deep end and pray that your body knows how to tread water when your brain doesn't. They say you'll live or you'll drown, but nobody tells you that you'll start to grieve what broke you. That you'll miss gasping for air and the taste of water in your lungs. Where familiarity lies, lives the comfort.

So settle in, the absence of pain will hurt for a while. This part will feel like the longest, but in retrospect, it is very short.

Because one day, someone will interlace their fingers with yours... and you will realize heartbreak left wounds upon your skin so that someone could show you their own scars and teach you how to stitch yourself back together.

Lightning Source UK Ltd.
Milton Keynes UK
UKHW040953021020
370914UK00001B/73